Liliuokalani
Queen of the Hawaiian Islands

S0-CQQ-798

Darleen Ramos

Boston, Massachusetts
Chandler, Arizona
Glenview, Illinois
Upper Saddle River, New Jersey

Illustrations
3 Joe LeMonnier; 5, 7, 13 Liz Zunon.

Photographs
Every effort has been made to secure permission and provide appropriate credit for photographic material.
The publisher deeply regrets any omission and pledges to correct errors called to its attention in subsequent editions.

Unless otherwise acknowledged, all photographs are the property of Pearson Education, Inc.

Photo locators denoted as follows: Top (T), Center (C), Bottom (B), Left (L), Right (R), Background (Bkgd)

Opener: Hawaii State Archives; 1 Hawaii State Archives; 2 Library of Congress; 4 Library of Congress; 8 Hawaii State Archives; 9 Hawaii State Archives; 10 Hawaii State Archives; 11 Hawaii State Archives; 12 Hawaii State Archives; 14 Photos to Go/Photolibrary; 15 Photos to Go/Photolibrary.

ISBN-13: 978-0-328-67625-5
ISBN-10:   0-328-67625-X

10 11 12 13 V0SI 18 17 16 15

Hawaii's Queen

Did you know that Hawaii was once a kingdom? It was ruled for most of its history by kings. Liliuokalani was Hawaii's first and only ruling queen. When Liliuokalani, or Liliu, was growing up in the 1800s, she learned about Hawaiian **culture**. She also learned about American and European cultures. Knowledge of both cultures helped prepare her to be queen.

Queen Liliuokalani's **reign** did not last long. There were many changes happening in Hawaii. Outsiders were moving to the islands and gaining control of the government. However, Liliuokalani believed Hawaii should be ruled by Hawaiians. She fought hard against the changes but was pushed out of power. Despite losing power, she continued to support Hawaiian culture and the Hawaiian people she loved.

Hawaiian History

Liliu Kamakaeha was born on September 2, 1838, in Honolulu. This city is on one of eight major islands making up the Hawaiian Islands. People have lived on the islands for about 1,500 years. The first people to come to Hawaii were from other Pacific islands. Those settlers created a Hawaiian culture. They built huge canoes and fished in the ocean. They enjoyed hula dancing and surfing. They had many gods. Kings and chiefs ruled the islands. The people enjoyed hula dances and surfing. The Hawaiians had no written language. They passed their history down to their children using a song called a chant. However, all this began to change as outsiders arrived.

The Hawaiian Islands

Kauai

Niihau

Oahu

Honolulu

Molokai

Lanai

Kahoolawe

Maui

Hawaii

PACIFIC OCEAN

Japan   U.S.

Hawaiian Islands

PACIFIC OCEAN

The first European to come to Hawaii was a British explorer named Captain James Cook. He sailed to the islands in 1778. Soon after, people all around the world learned about the beautiful Hawaiian Islands and the people who lived there. It wasn't long before others came to Hawaii.

In 1820, **missionaries** from the United States came to the islands. They taught Hawaiians about the Christian religion. Slowly things began to change. The American missionaries **outlawed** hula dancing. They encouraged Hawaiians to wear American style clothing instead of their own traditional clothes. The missionaries created a written language based on the sounds of the Hawaiian language. Hawaiians learned how to read and write their own language. They could now pass down their history with writing.

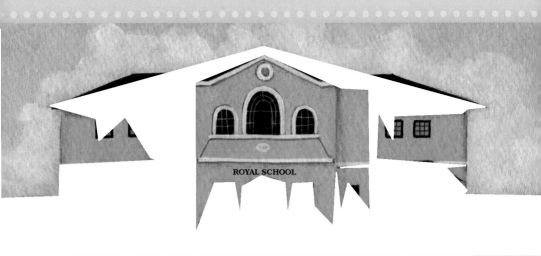

ROYAL SCHOOL

A Royal Child

Because of the missionaries, Liliuokalani was born into a kingdom that was a mix of both Hawaiian and American cultures. Her parents were powerful chiefs on the islands. People celebrated with chants on the day she was born.

Little Liliu was adopted by two other chiefs. It was a Hawaiian custom that **royal** children like Liliu be raised by two chiefs other than her parents. This custom created a strong bond of friendship among the chiefs. At age four, Liliu started going to a school run by American missionaries. It was called the Royal School. She went to the school with other royal children.

Liliuokalani learned many things about American culture from the missionaries who ran the Royal School. She was taught to read and write English. She was also taught to dress and behave like an American. Liliu's favorite

subject was music. She could easily read musical notes, and she even wrote her own songs.

Many years later, Liliu wrote a book about her life. It was called *Hawaii's Story by Hawaii's Queen*. In it, she talked about how Hawaiians loved to tell about their history through song. While the missionaries had outlawed some of the traditional chants, Liliu never forgot about her culture. She wrote more than 150 chants and other songs throughout her life. She wrote songs in both American and Hawaiian styles.

Learning to Be Queen

Liliuokalani kept busy after her school years were over. She went to royal events. She also traveled to the different Hawaiian Islands to learn more about the kingdom. On one trip, she visited a volcano that was no longer active. She slept in a tent right at the edge of the crater!

For a short time, Liliu planned to marry a Hawaiian prince. However, she married an American named John Dominis instead. The wedding took place in 1862. Liliu was 24 years old. All of the chiefs came to see her get married. After the wedding, Liliu and her husband moved into a huge house in Honolulu called Washington Place.

Washington Place

In 1874, Liliuokalani's brother, David Kalakaua, became the king of Hawaii. He named Liliuokalani to be his **heir**. In 1881, King Kalakaua went on a trip around the world. Liliuokalani was left in charge while he was gone.

At the time, much of the world's sugar cane came from Hawaii. The kingdom had a great need for people to work on the huge sugar cane **plantations**. Many workers came by ship from China and Japan. Soon after Liliu's brother left, a ship arrived with thousands of Chinese workers. Some of them had smallpox. The disease spread quickly and many Hawaiians died.

A sugar plantation.

Then Liliuokalani made a bold move. She closed all the **ports** to all ships coming from or going to Hawaii. She did this to protect Hawaiians. She did not want the disease to spread more than it had. However, the American owners of the plantations were not happy. Closing the ports to ships meant they could not sell sugar cane. It also meant they would lose money. The plantation owners complained.

Liliuokalani did not however, change her mind. Because of her actions, the disease did not spread much beyond Honolulu. In total, about 800 people in the city got smallpox. About 300 people died. Without Liliu's decision, the number of deaths could have been far greater.

A Trip Overseas

In 1887 Liliuokalani's brother, the king, suggested that Liliuokalani take a trip around the world. Great Britain's Queen Victoria was celebrating her fiftieth year as queen. Liliuokalani would go to the celebration and meet

Liliuokalani at the time of Queen Victoria's celebration

the queen. Liliu was excited about the trip. On the way, she visited several states in the United States. She also met President Grover Cleveland.

Liliuokalani saw many new things on this trip. For the first time, she saw snow and bare trees without leaves. In Britain, Liliu saw old castles and heard church bells. The music was much different from the Hawaiian music back home.

Liliuokalani met royalty from many other countries as well. She was treated with great respect because she was also from a royal family.

Trouble in Hawaii

While Liliuokalani was gone, the king faced troubles at home. For many years, American businessmen had been coming to Hawaii to build sugar cane and pineapple plantations. The plantation owners became wealthy. They held powerful jobs in the government too. Each year, the businessmen took more power from the king.

King Kalakaua knew the Hawaiian people were not making money from the plantations. He wanted to limit the power of the American businessmen. The business owners feared the king would write laws that would hurt their businesses. In 1887, they forced the king— at gunpoint—to sign a new constitution. A constitution is a document that includes basic laws for a nation.

King Kalakaua

The new constitution gave most of the power to the businessmen. Native Hawaiians no longer had the right to vote. Liliuokalani was upset with this change. She believed her country and culture were being destroyed.

Over the next few years, the king lost even more power. Then in 1891, he became ill. He sailed to California to get medical treatment. He died while he was there. On January 29, 1891, Liliuokalani became Hawaii's first ruling queen. Hawaiians hoped the new queen would bring power back to the Hawaiians.

Liliuokalani during her reign

Losing Power

The American business owners did not want to give power back to the Hawaiian people. They wanted the United States to **annex** Hawaii instead. If that happened, the queen would lose all her power. Hawaii would no longer be a kingdom. However,

American soldiers in Hawaii

the queen had her own plans. She wrote a new constitution. It would return all the power to the kingdom. It would also give back voting rights to the Hawaiian people. For two years, the queen tried to restore Hawaiian rights and customs.

Although Queen Liliuokalani worked hard, she did not succeed. When powerful businessmen learned about the new constitution, they contacted a United States official in Hawaii. He ordered a nearby American warship to send in soldiers. The soldiers landed on shore with guns and cannons.

The queen was imprisoned in Iolani Palace.

Queen Liliuokalani did not want anyone to be killed. Therefore, on January 17, 1893, she gave up the throne. She watched as the American flag flew over Iolani Palace, once her home. Her only hope was to ask President Cleveland to help.

Cleveland ordered the businessmen to **reinstate** the queen, but they refused. In 1895, the Hawaiian people rose up against the new government. They wanted the queen back in power. When the **uprising** failed, the government arrested the queen. She stood trial and was found guilty for working against the new government. Hawaiians were heartbroken. Their kingdom was no more.

The New Hawaii

Queen Liliuokalani was locked up for eight months. Afterward, she went to live at Washington Place. In 1898, the United States annexed Hawaii. Liliuokalani spent her last years sharing her love of Hawaiian culture with others. During this time, she wrote her most famous song, "Aloha 'Oe." It is a song about hope. In 1917, she died at age 79.

In 1959, Hawaii became a state in the United States. Today, people from all over the world visit Hawaii to explore its beauty and learn about its culture. People enjoy surfing, traditional chants, and hula dancing, which is no longer against the law. Some Hawaiians still speak the Hawaiian language. And Queen Liliuokalani is remembered as a person who fought to defend her kingdom and culture.

This statue in Hawaii honors Queen Liliuokalani.

Glossary

annex to take over; to add a country or territory to another country

culture the way of life of a group of people

heir a person who takes over a title or ownership of property after someone dies

missionary a person who teaches his or her religion to others

outlaw to make something against the rules or the law

plantation large farm with many workers

port a place where ships stop to load or unload goods

reign the time in which a queen or king rules

reinstate to return someone to power

royal having to do with a king or queen

uprising a revolt